WAR AND CONFLICT IN THE MIDDLE EAST™

THE IRAN-IRAQ WAR

EDWARD WILLETT

THE ROSEN PUBLISHING GROUP, INC., NEW YORK

Published in 2004 by The Rosen Publishing Group, Inc.
29 East 21st Street, New York, NY 10010

First Edition

Library of Congress Cataloging-in-Publication Data

Willett, Edward, 1959–
The Iran-Iraq War / by Edward Willett. — 1st ed.
    p. cm. — (War and conflict in the Middle East)
Summary: Examines the history behind the longest war of the twentieth
century, which raged between Iran and Iraq in the 1980s, and looks at
its ongoing ramifications.
Includes bibliographical references and index.
ISBN 0-8239-4547-2
1. Iran-Iraq War, 1980–1988—Juvenile literature. [1. Iran-Iraq War,
1980–1988.]
I. Title. II. Series.
DS318.85.W55 2003
955.05'42—dc22

                                        2003014000

Manufactured in the United States of America

CONTENTS

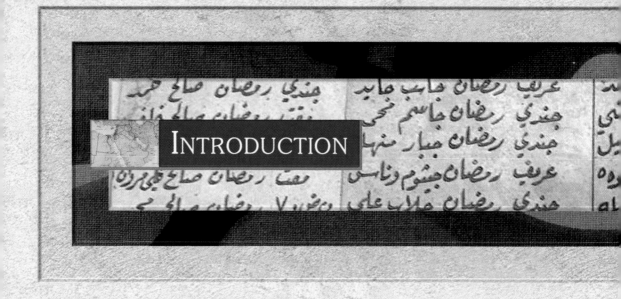

On September 22, 1980, Iraq invaded its neighboring country of Iran. Iraqi president Saddam Hussein wanted and expected a short war. Instead, the Iran-Iraq War became the longest war of the twentieth century. It was also one of the bloodiest. Over eight years, as many as one million people may have been killed. Hundreds of thousands more were wounded. Millions became refugees. Many casualties were caused by Iraqi chemical weapons used throughout the war. The total economic cost of the war has been estimated at $400 billion.

At first, the war was seen as little concern to other countries. But much of the world's oil comes from the Persian Gulf. Beginning in 1984, tankers from many different nations were attacked by both Iran and Iraq. As a result, the United States Navy began escorting ships in the gulf. As the war progressed, U.S. forces destroyed several

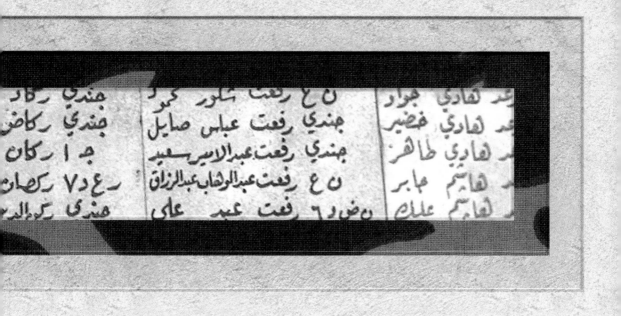

Iranian ships and naval platforms, and inadvertently shot down an Iranian airliner.

When the fighting finally ended in 1988, little had changed. Iran and Iraq's borders remained the same. The two leaders, Saddam Hussein in Iraq and Ayatollah Khomeini in Iran, remained in power. Since then, events of that region have echoed the destructive war between Iran and Iraq.

CHAPTER 1

THE STAGE IS SET

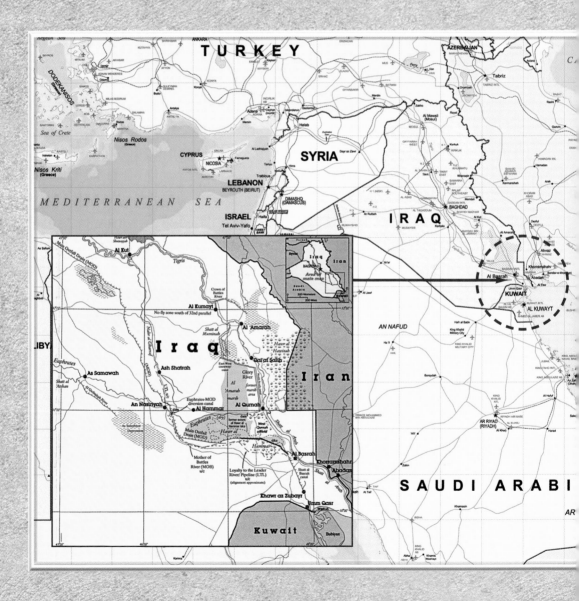

Iran and Iraq have had their share of conflicts through the ages. One long-standing dispute has been over the 127-mile-long (204.4-kilometer-long) Shatt al Arab river. This important waterway separates the two countries at the head of the Persian Gulf. Both Iran and Iraq have important ports on the Shatt al Arab. For Iraq, the river is the only outlet to the Persian Gulf and the shipping lanes it needs to export oil.

Historically, Iraq has tried to claim the entire river (and both banks), while Iran has claimed half of it. A 1937 treaty fixed the border at the low watermark on the eastern side of the river, except for the area near the important Iranian ports of Abadan and Khorramshahr. There, the frontier was set at the *thalweg*, or the central deepest part of the river.

The 1937 treaty seemed to mark a new beginning in Iran-Iraq relations. That same year, the two countries agreed to work together in a regional alliance with Turkey and Afghanistan. In 1955, Iran and Iraq joined Britain, Turkey, and Pakistan in the Central Treaty Organization for regional defense. Soon, though, relations between the countries deteriorated. Internal struggles between political parties and the people were changing the politics of both countries.

Iran and Iraq share a border 795 miles (1,280 km) long. Treaties had always kept peace between the countries. This changed after oil became the cash resource for both countries.

Iranian Coups and Power Struggles

In 1953, the leader of the Iranian parliament led a coup (an overthrow of the government) against Shah Mohammad Reza Pahlavi. Pahlavi was briefly deposed as ruler of Iran. With the help of other countries, especially the United States, he was quickly restored to power. One reason for the coup, and for his quick restoration, was his policy of granting foreign companies control over Iranian oil.

The Central Treaty Organization (also known as the Baghdad Pact) was formed in 1955 among Iraq, Turkey, Pakistan, Iran, Britain, and the United States. Above, representatives of the Baghdad Pact nations gather together in 1956 to discuss the Israeli presence in Egypt.

The shah became even more pro-Western after his return to power. He also became more and more dictatorial. This turned many of his own people against him. Conservative Muslims considered Western ways evil and corrupt. They thought this of all countries that did not live by religious rules. Meanwhile, nationalists wanted to see Iranians control their own resources. Oil sales and Western support enabled the shah to strengthen his hold on Iran. With oil money, he built a very powerful modern military.

Iraqi Baathists Take Control

The pro-Western Iraqi government would not have the same luck as the shah of Iran. In 1958, military officers overthrew the pro-Western monarchy in Iraq. Abdul Karim Kassem, a nationalist republican, took over. He was strongly opposed to foreign influence in the region. The 1958 coup was followed by another coup in 1963. The military and the Baath Socialist Party performed this government overthrow.

The Baathists combined socialist economic principles with the dream of uniting all Arabs under a single government. Later that year, Abd al-Salam Arif threw the Baathists out of the new government. This was an odd event, since Arif had been the leader of the Baath Party. Just five years later, yet another coup, led by Ahmad Hasan Bakr, returned the Baath Party to power. This time the Baathists would stay in power. What hurt the Baathists—and the Iraqi people—was their anti-Western stance. They didn't get any help from Western governments, nor did they trade heavily with them at the time. This kept Iraq economically and militarily weak. Just as Iran was building its power and wealth, Iraq was falling behind.

Tensions Are Raised

Confident in its new strength, Iran reopened talks on the division of the Shatt al Arab in 1959. Iran wanted the border to be the thalweg for the river's entire length. Ten years of negotiations accomplished nothing. Finally, in April 1969, Iran withdrew from the 1937 treaty and refused to pay the Iraqi tolls for use of the waterway. Iran sent a merchant ship, with a naval escort, through the disputed part of the river on April 24. Tensions grew. Both countries sent military forces to the river-banks. They stood on opposite sides of the river, waiting.

Tensions were also raised over the next few years by Iranian support for various antigovernment forces within Iraq. Iranians especially helped the Kurds. Historically, Iranians are Persians, Iraqis are Arabs, and the Kurds are a third distinct group, with their own culture. The Kurds never had an independent country. Many Kurds wanted to change that.

The Kurdish Independence Movement

The Kurdish independence movement threatened Iraq's survival. Two-thirds of its oil production came from Kurdish territory. The area also contained Iraq's most fertile wheat-growing land.

With Iranian support, the Kurds launched a full-scale war to fight for their independence. This civil war devastated Iraq's economy and almost destroyed its government. Iran's help for the Kurds almost pushed it into war with Iraq as early as 1974.

Neither country, however, felt it could afford an all-out war. Secretly, they approached the Algerian government to try and settle the reasons for war. In March 1975, Iran and Iraq signed the Algiers Accord. They agreed to halt fighting. Iran agreed to withdraw its support for the Kurdish rebels. Iraq agreed to give up its long-standing land claim over the Iranian area of Khuzestan. Iraq also agreed to make the thalweg of the

Disheartened Kurdish troops stand in Rawanduz at the Iraq border after Iran's decision to withdraw its support for the Kurdish struggle for independence from Iraq. There are approximately 25 million Kurds in Iraq, Iran, Turkey, and Syria. Kurds have been struggling for a century to create their own nation, Kurdistan.

Shatt al Arab the border between the two countries. For the next few years, relations between Iran and Iraq remained calm. Political changes in both countries soon altered this peace.

Revolution in Iran

A worldwide recession (economic slump) in the 1970s reduced the world's demand for oil, which decreased the price for oil. Iran's economy suffered. The people against the shah were now even angrier. Anti-shah demonstrations were violently put down by the military. This led to more violence.

The spiritual leader of the anti-shah movement was Ayatollah Ruhollah Khomeini. Khomeini had already been exiled once from Iran, in 1964, for anti-shah activities. Yet, in the mid-1970s, he still held enormous influence over people. Khomeini taught that Islamic principles should rule the governing of Iran as well as its religious life. Khomeini's exile had taken him to Najaf, one of the holy cities of Shiite Islam. (Ironically, Najaf is in Iraq.) From there, his sermons and writings were secretly but widely distributed in Iran.

The Algiers Accord included a commitment from each country to stop helping dissidents in the other's country. Khomeini was therefore expelled from Iraq in 1978 at the shah's request. Khomeini went to Paris. There he became an even more powerful anti-shah figure because he could more easily communicate with his supporters. He also drew the attention of the world media.

Demonstrations against the shah swelled through 1979. The demonstrators began calling for Khomeini's

Two Branches of Islam

One of the roots of the Iran-Iraq conflict is the ancient split in Islam between Sunnism and Shiism. When the prophet Muhammad, founder of Islam, died in 632, his family believed that his cousin and son-in-law, Ali, should become the next leader. Others felt the leader should be chosen from the wider community of believers. This second group won the dispute. They founded the Umayyad dynasty and practiced what today is known as Sunnism.

Those who believed Ali should have been the leader did not accept the Umayyad leaders or their Sunni practices. Often, followers of Ali gave up their lives for that belief. Today, this group represents the minority branch of Islam, the Shiites. The majority of Shiites are Twelvers, so called because they recognize twelve imams (leaders). The first was Ali. The twelfth imam, called the Hidden Imam, disappeared in 873 but, they believe, will return as the Mahdi (messiah).

Only about 15 percent of the world's Muslims are Shiite. In Iran, however, they are the majority. Twelver Shiism became the state religion in Iran in the sixteenth century. Shiite Muslims also form a slight majority in Iraq. The holiest Shiite cities are located in Iraq.

return from exile. On January 16, 1979, the shah, seriously ill with cancer, left Iran for good. On February 1, 1979, Khomeini returned and set about creating the world's first Islamic state. Khomeini cut Iran's ties with the West. He called Western governments "thieves" and "evil." He often called the United States "the Great Satan."

Khomeini had equally harsh feelings for the Iraqi government. The Baath Party did not base its policies on Islamic principles. The Iraqi government also oppressed its Shiite population. These differences—and disputes—would soon thrust the two nations into war. The driving force behind the war was Saddam Hussein. Shortly after Khomeini took power in Iran, Saddam Hussein took control of Iraq.

Saddam Hussein Takes Over Iraq

Hussein had been a member of the Baathist Party since 1955, when he was eighteen years old. After the 1958

Iraqi president Saddam Hussein and Cuban vice president Raul Castro mingle with other leaders at the first meeting of the countries of the Non-Aligned Movement in Havana, Cuba, in September 1979. Member countries felt it wasn't necessary to align themselves with capitalists (United States) or Communists (Soviet Union).

revolution, he was wounded while fighting for the Baathists against the government. He fled the country for fear of being sent to jail. He returned after the 1963 revolution, but he was forced into hiding when the Baathists were purged from government. Eventually, he became the assistant secretary general of the Baath Party and the head of the Baath militia.

When Ahmad Hasan Bakr seized power in 1968, Hussein was well placed to advance. He had a reputation for ruthlessness and efficiency. Also, Bakr was his kinsman. They had both come from Tikrit, a town northeast of Baghdad.

Hussein helped unite the Baath Party's rule. Among other things, he oversaw the arrests of thousands of opposition figures. Many were killed in televised executions. By 1975, Hussein was second in command of Iraq.

When Khomeini returned to Iran and launched his revolution, Hussein was concerned it would take root in Iraq's Shiite majority. Large antigovernment demonstrations by Shiites in June 1979 seemed to confirm the potential threat. Hussein gave Bakr a list of dissidents he thought should be executed. The list included many military officers. Bakr did not want to execute military officers. Most of the government officials sided with Hussein. Bakr was placed under house arrest. Later, he resigned (officially, for health reasons). Saddam Hussein quickly seized power.

Hussein was afraid Iran would export its revolution into his country. Ayatollah Khomeini thought Saddam Hussein was an evil infidel. The stage was set for war.

CHAPTER 2

IRAQ ATTACKS

In June 1979, Khomeini's new government began urging the Iraqi population to overthrow the Baath regime. A few months later, Iran resumed supporting Kurdish rebels in Iraq. It also provided aid to underground Shiite movements. These organizations launched terrorist attacks against Iraqi government officials.

On April 1, 1980, the underground Shiites tried unsuccessfully to assassinate Tariq Aziz, the Iraqi deputy premier. Two weeks later, they attempted to assassinate the Iraqi minister of 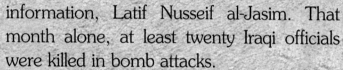 information, Latif Nusseif al-Jasim. That month alone, at least twenty Iraqi officials were killed in bomb attacks.

Hussein had no choice but to fight back. He executed a prominent Shiite cleric, Ayatollah Sadr. Sadr's sister was also executed. This outraged Khomeini and infuriated the Iranian people. Hussein also expelled as many as 100,000 Iraqi Shiites. In addition, he provided support for rebellious Kurds and Arabs within Iran.

On March 8, 1980, Iran announced it was withdrawing its ambassador from Iraq. All of its diplomats were gone from Baghdad by April 7.

Hussein Sees a Weakened Iran

Internal dissent and purges in Iran had greatly weakened the Iranian military. Its

Kurdish troops ready for battle in Iran in 1979. In the early 1980s, Kurdish troops launched a large-scale campaign against Iran, Turkey, and Iraq in hopes of winning back their homeland.

spurning of the West and the seizing of the American embassy and taking of hostages by militant students had lost the country's support of its traditional military arms suppliers. Meanwhile, Iraq's economy was booming, and its government was firmly in Hussein's hands. For Hussein, it appeared there could be no better time to attack Iran. A successful campaign could end the threat of a Shiite revolution within Iraq. It could also secure the Shatt al Arab once and for all.

Iraqi Kurds are executed by Saddam Hussein's army because they have fought for their freedom and an independent state. Iran encouraged Iraqi dissidents, just as Iraq encouraged dissident groups in Iran to revolt against Ayatollah Khomeini's reign.

Hussein also wanted to become a major leader within the Arab world. For twenty-five years, Egypt had been the leader among the Arab nations. But Egypt had recently been suspended from the Arab League for signing a peace accord with Israel. If Hussein could "liberate" the Arabs living in the Iranian province of Khuzestan, Iraq would surely be the new leading Arab power. This move would also greatly expand Iraq's coastline and deprive Iran of its largest source of oil.

By August 1980, military clashes along the border had escalated. Now tank and artillery duels happened frequently. Air strikes also became common. On September 2, Iraqi and Iranian troops clashed near Qasr-e Shirin. On September 4, Iran shelled two Iraqi towns, Khanaqin and Mandali. Baghdad claimed Iran had also bombed the two towns and their oil installations.

On September 6, Iraq called on Iran to hand over 115 to 145 square miles (298 to 376 square kilometers) of land it claimed belonged to it under an unpublished clause of the Algiers Accord. In response, Iran shelled more Iraqi border towns. Four days later, Iraq announced that it had taken the disputed territory from Iran. The lack of Iranian resistance must have helped convince Hussein that the time was ripe for an all-out assault.

On September 14, the Iranian military announced that Iran would no longer agree to the borders set out in the Algiers Accord. On September 17, Hussein, in a televised speech to the recently elected Iraqi National Assembly, publicly tore up Iraq's copies of the Algiers Accord. He then

Iraqi and Iranian Forces at the Beginning of the War

Iraq	Iran
Ground Forces	**Ground Forces**
Regular Army, Active	Regular Army, Active
200,000	150,000
Regular Army, Reserves	Regular Army, Reserves
250,000	400,000
Other Forces	**Other Forces**
Popular Army (paramilitary)	Popular Army (paramilitary)
250,000	250,000
Battle Tanks	Battle Tanks
2,500	1,740
Armored Fighting Vehicles	Armored Fighting Vehicles
2,000	1,075
Major Artillery	Major Artillery
1,000	1,000
Air Forces	**Air Forces**
Regular Air Force	Regular Air Force
38,000	70,000
Combat Aircraft	Combat Aircraft
335	445
Combat Helicopters	Combat Helicopters
40	500
Total Helicopters	Total Helicopters
250	750
Naval Forces	**Naval Forces**
Regular Navy	Regular Navy
4,250	36,000

ordered any Iranian ships using the Shatt al Arab to use Iraqi pilots and fly the Iraqi flag. Iran refused. Heavy fighting broke out along the river. Iran called up reserves on September 20. On the night of September 22, Iraq attacked Iran with heavy forces.

The War Begins

The first hours of all-out war saw two waves of Iraqi MiG-23 and MiG-21 aircraft attack ten Iranian air bases. Two bases were near the Iranian capital city of Tehran. Iraq's goal was to destroy parked Iranian aircraft and to wreck runways. For the most part, the attack failed. Many bombs missed their targets or misfired. Many of the Iranian combat planes sat protected in armored shelters. Within hours, Iranian F-4 Phantoms took off from the bombed bases and successfully attacked strategic targets near major Iraqi cities.

Hussein quickly realized that the Iranian air force was still functioning. He also knew that his air bases were all within reach of Iranian forces. To protect his small air force fleet, Hussein scattered most of his combat aircraft to friendly nations in the region. The Iraqi air force thus played a small role in the invasion after that first day's assault.

Early on the morning of September 23, six Iraqi divisions—thousands of soldiers—crossed the border into Iran along a 400-mile-long (644-km-long) front. A mechanized division overran the Iranian border garrison at Qasr-e Shirin. This move blocked a possible counterattack against Baghdad, just 75 miles (121 km) away. Another division entered Iran in the central southern region. However, the main target was the province of Khuzestan in the south. The military goals included capturing Ahvaz, a major military base. Also on the military's list of objectives were Khorramshahr and Abadan. Iraq had to capture these two ports to secure the Shatt al Arab.

The lightning-like attack and the light Iranian resistance convinced many people that Iraq would win the war in weeks. Most of what little resistance was offered came from the Iranian Revolutionary Guard Corps. This was a lightly armed

An Iraqi soldier takes cover during the Iran-Iraq War in 1980. In the early stages of the war, Iran had weak defenses. Iraq took advantage of its vulnerability and invaded on September 22, 1980.

militia force made up of fervent believers in Khomeini's revolution. It fought fiercely, especially in built-up areas.

Iraq's Success and Iran's Defiance

On September 25, Baghdad announced that it had laid siege to several major cities, including Ahvaz and Khorramshahr. That same day, it shelled the world's largest oil refinery at Abadan. Iran responded with a 140-plane assault on Iraq's oil facilities. With the damage mounting, both countries suspended oil shipments on September 26.

Hussein did not let his forces advance as far as they could. Instead, on September 28 he announced that his territorial objectives had been achieved. He said he was willing to accept a cease-fire, if Iran accepted Iraq's complete rights over the Shatt al Arab and the other disputed territory. Iran also had to "abandon its evil attempts to interfere in the domestic affairs of the region's countries."

Iran refused. The war intensified. Iraq attempted to overrun the cities it had laid siege to. Hussein had told his forces that the Arabs living in Khuzestan would rise up and greet them as liberators. Instead, the Khuzestanis fought back. Trucks and other vehicles that evacuated women and children from the embattled cities returned loaded with volunteers. In Khorramshahr alone, each side suffered about 7,000 dead and seriously wounded. The Iraqis also lost more than 100 tanks and armored vehicles.

Iraqi forces entered Khorramshahr on October 24, but the city wasn't fully in their hands until November 10. By that time, Iraqis and Iranians alike were calling it Khunistan, which means "City of Blood."

Battles and Stalemate

The capture of Khorramshahr was Iraq's greatest achievement of the early stages of the war. On December 7, 1980, Saddam Hussein announced that Iraq had settled into a defensive posture. For the next eight months, the two sides mostly exchanged artillery fire and air raids across the battlefront. There were also small-scale raids by ground forces.

Iran did attempt one counterattack, on January 5, 1981. The Iranians plunged deep into the Iraqi lines but could not break through. As a result, the attackers were encircled. The resulting tank battle, one of the largest of the war, destroyed approximately 100 of Iran's American-made tanks. Another 150 were captured. Iraq lost only 50 of its Soviet-made tanks.

Behind the lines, Iraq was trying to create new infantry units and working on infrastructure. For example, it built a paved highway from the city of Basra to the front lines so it could more easily supply its forces. Iran, meanwhile, flooded some areas of countryside to make them unusable by Iraqi troops. The purge of the Iranian military ended. Reservists were called up, training intensified, and forces were regrouped and sent to the front lines.

Iran also managed to locate a source of weapons and spare parts: Vietnam. The U.S. military had left behind thousands of weapons and spare parts when it abandoned Vietnam in the mid-1970s. A few other anti-Western countries, including Libya, Syria, and North Korea, also provided supplies to Iran.

Much of the Iranian government's energy was focused on internal problems, not the war. In June 1981, Khomeini removed from power the country's first president and commander in chief, Abol Hassan Bani-Sadr. Soon after, Bani-Sadr fled the country. Demonstrations that followed his removal were brutally suppressed. On June 28, someone bombed the revolutionary party headquarters in Tehran, killing more than seventy revolutionary leaders. More arrests and executions followed. So did more bombings. Bani-Sadr's replacement, Mohammad Ali Raja'i, was one of those killed.

On October 20, 1981, Hojaat al-Islam Ali Khamenei took over as president. Khamenei would remain president for the rest of the war. Supreme power, however, still rested with Ayatollah Khomeini. When the internal strife finally began to ease, Iran once again turned its full attention to the Iraqi invaders on its soil.

CHAPTER 3

IRAN STRIKES BACK

In late September 1981, Iran launched a number of diversionary attacks in various parts of Khuzestan. Iraq responded by sending some of the forces bombing Abadan to other areas. Then, on September 27, Iran attacked the now-depleted forces near Abadan. Two infantry divisions and some Iranian Revolutionary Guard Corps units pushed outside the city against the surrounding Iraqi army. Armor and artillery units supported the attackers. The fighting was fierce and bloody. After many hours of battle, the Iranians successfully pushed the Iraqis back, ending the city's siege.

An Iranian Advantage

The defeat demoralized Iraqi troops. Suddenly discipline problems and desertions hurt Iraqi formations. Iran followed up with more attacks. A major offensive called Operation Jerusalem Way took place from November 29 to December 7. This time the fighting took place in the mud and rain. Once again Iran proved victorious. It reclaimed the town of Bostan.

Operation Jerusalem Way proved that the Iranian military forces were now better organized. It also marked the first use of a new method of attack. It was designed to counteract the advantages of the better-equipped Iraqi forces. The Iranian

Jubilant Iranians gather together to celebrate the recapturing of a vital position during the Iran-Iraq War. In this counteroffensive in 1982, Iran was able to take back most of what it lost during the first two years of the war.

Young, battle-weary Iranian soldiers trek across the newly regained territory as more troops line up behind them. Because the war was so long, resources and manpower soon became scarce. Often, those who were too young or too old were sent into battle.

Revolutionary Guard Corps attacked heavily fortified Iraqi positions in a series of "human waves," without artillery or air support. Huge numbers of Iranian soldiers simply attacked overland against Iraqi positions. They took heavy casualties but overwhelmed the defenders through sheer numbers.

In February 1982, Iraq told Iran that it was willing to withdraw from Iran in stages. This would take place even before a peace agreement was reached. However, negotiations would have to begin and make progress. Not long afterward, Saddam Hussein said he was willing to withdraw from Iran as long as Iraq received assurances that such a withdrawal would lead to a negotiated settlement.

Iran ignored both offers and continued attacking Iraqi positions. On March 22, Iran launched Operation Undeniable Victory, the largest campaign up to that time. More than 100,000 troops were involved on each side. A surprise night attack by armored units was followed by human wave attacks.

In a typical human wave attack during that campaign, 1,000 men, each armed with a shoulder-held rocket launcher, would storm the Iraqi positions. Another 1,000 would follow 200 to 500 yards (183 to 457 meters) behind the first, another 1,000 after that, and so on. As Robin Wright describes it in her book, *In the Name of God: The Khomeini Decade*, "After one column . . . dropped, it was followed by another group of frenzied troops, usually urged on by mullahs [religious leaders] attached to each unit."

In April and May 1982, more Iranian offensives followed. The Iranians were now overwhelming the Iraqis. They

Human Waves of Children

The first "human wave" attacks used Iranian Revolutionary Guard Corps soldiers. Many who took part in later human wave attacks were boys aged ten through sixteen. These were volunteers from the Basij organization. Basij was originally formed as a civil defense force.

Most of the boys came from peasant and working-class families. Recruiting mullahs visited these boys' schools looking for volunteers. There was also a huge media campaign. In one television ad, a young boy talked about how wonderful it was to be fighting for Islam against the Iraqis. Then he cursed the Iraqis and all Arabs, saying they were not good Muslims and called on other boys to join him in the war.

Many boys left their homes and schools to join, sometimes without the permission of their parents. They were sent onto the battlefield without much training. They were equipped with only a rifle and a couple of hand grenades, and they were told to charge Iraqi positions. Often they were sent over minefields. By detonating the mines, the boys cleared the way for the Iranian Revolutionary Guard Corps to follow. Thousands of these boys were killed or captured over the course of the war.

recaptured their town of Khorramshahr. In all, from November to May, Iranian forces recaptured more than 3,000 square miles (7,770 sq km) of territory. This represented about one-third of what Iraq had seized in its original invasion.

Hussein's Olive Branch?

On June 6, 1982, Israel invaded Lebanon. Hussein saw an opportunity to save face and his army. He offered Iran a cease-fire so both Iraqi and Iranian troops could aid the Palestinians caught up in war in Beirut, Lebanon. On June 20, Hussein announced that his troops had begun to withdraw from Iran and would be gone within ten days.

In an interview published in 1996, Ayatollah Khomeini's son Ahmad said that Khomeini "wanted to stop the war after the liberation of Khorramshahr, but those in charge . . . said we should advance to the Shatt al Arab

During the invasion of Lebanon in 1982, Israeli tanks made their way to Beirut. Israel offered its support to Iran, thinking of Iraq as a greater enemy to the state of Israel. Also, many Jews resided in Iran, and Israel hoped that its support of Iran would secure their safety.

bank so that we would be in a position to demand reparations. The Imam [Khomeini] was against it. He replied that 'if you continue the war and do not succeed, this war will never end. Now is the best time to end the war.'"

Nevertheless, Iran again rejected Iraq's peace offering. Iran's peace terms now included the equivalent of $150 billion. Additional demands included the return of the 100,000 Shiites expelled from Iraq before the war and the overthrow of Saddam Hussein.

On a grassy plane along the Khorramshahr front, Iranian forces get ready for liftoff in 1983. Thanks to their air force bombers' superior ammunition capacity, Iranians were able to fight aggressively at the beginning of the war.

On July 13, Iranian forces advanced inside Iraq for the first time in the largest infantry battle since the Second World War. The battle saw 130,000 troops fighting at one time. However, Iraq's defense within its own borders was much stronger than it had been in Iran. Iran had moved only a short distance, while suffering heavy casualties.

Attack and Counterattack

Iran launched more offensives into Iraq in the autumn of 1982. However, the human wave assaults that had successfully driven the Iraqis from Iran were often repulsed within Iraq. In defense of their own country, Iraqi soldiers proved to be fierce fighters. The story was the same in 1983, when Iran launched three major offensives, all of which used the human wave approach, and all of which failed.

On February 6, 1983, Tehran launched Operation Dawn in an attempt to capture the strategic highway between Basra and Baghdad. Approximately 100,000 Iranian troops marched many miles into Iraq. Iraqi warplanes and helicopter gunships pushed them back. In the end, Iran recovered only about 100 square miles (259 sq km) of territory.

The Iraqi victory prompted Iraq's military leaders to launch their own offensive in the central sector. A huge battle near the town of Miqdadiya took place weeks later, but Iran fought it off with no difficulty. In April, Iran tried again to seize the Basra-Baghdad highway. Again, Iraq fought back with warplanes and attack helicopters, and again Iran suffered heavy losses.

Arms from Abroad

Both Iran and Iraq had to buy most of their weapons from foreign countries. Iraq found it easier to get weaponry than Iran. To begin with, the Soviet Union was a longtime ally of Iraq. Over the course of the war, the Soviets sold the Iraqis hundreds of tanks, scores of jet fighters and bombers (including ultramodern MiG-29s with the latest electronics), and surface-to-air and surface-to-surface missiles.

The French provided Iraq with $5.6 billion of weapons during the first two years of the war alone. The equipment included fighters, helicopters, tanks, self-propelled guns, missiles, and electronic equipment. Iraq owed France billions of dollars, and France felt Hussein's regime had to be kept in power to pay off that debt.

Egypt provided spare parts and ammunition, plus tanks and bombers. Spain provided light and heavy military vehicles. Brazil sold Iraq armored personnel carriers. Italy sold Iraq naval supplies. Britain provided parts for British tanks captured from the Iranians.

In February 1982, the United States removed Iraq from its list of states supporting international terrorism. This allowed for more trade between the countries. The United States did this because Iran appeared to be winning the war. By November 1984, the United States began supplying Iraq with military intelligence. Washington also gave Iraq hundreds of millions of dollars in credit for food products and agricultural equipment.

Iran didn't have as much international support, but it did manage to get help from Libya, Syria, and North Korea. They sold Iran artillery pieces, antiaircraft weapons, and antitank missiles. Britain provided spare parts for tanks and other armored vehicles in 1985. China, Taiwan, Argentina, South Africa, Pakistan, and Switzerland also contributed arms, munitions, and spare parts. Even Israel, which hoped to improve relations with Iran, provided critical parts such as tires for F-4 jets and spare parts for tanks.

One disadvantage the Iranians faced was the fact that Iraq had access to information from United States intelligence satellites. The United States backed Iraq all through the war. It gave Iraq intelligence reports through Saudi Arabia. Iraq learned where Iranian forces were and when they moved to a new location. This meant the Iranians couldn't concentrate forces in an area prior to an attack for fear the satellites would spot them.

In July 1983, Iran launched a third offensive, along the route from Piranshahr in Iran to Rawandoz in Iraq. This time the objective was to retake Iranian land. Rebel Iraqi Kurds and Shiites aided Iranian troops. The forces penetrated 9 miles (14.5 km) into Iraq. They took two major strategic targets, the peak of Mount Karman and the garrison town of Hajj Umran. This time, thanks in part to the mountainous terrain, they were able to hang on to their gains. The use of the Iraqi rebels was part of Tehran's new strategy to destabilize Saddam Hussein's regime.

Finally, on July 30, 1983, Iran successfully captured and held 60 sq miles (155 sq km) of territory, half of it within Iraq, in the central section of the border.

The only place Iraq really had any success over these months was at sea. In the first half of December 1982, Iraq claimed to have sunk six Iranian merchant and naval vessels. In January 1983, Iraq attacked the Nowruz oil rig in the northern Persian Gulf. In February and March, Iraq used air and naval strikes to damage Iranian installations. Both sides lost naval ships in these battles. The battle had spilled into the important shipping lanes of the Persian Gulf.

By early 1983, Iraq had lost 117 warplanes. Nevertheless, it was able to maintain an edge in air attacks because it continued to receive new aircraft from France and Egypt (which provided Chinese-made MiG-19s and MiG-21s).

The Political War Heats Up

The successes of the Iranian forces alarmed not only Saddam Hussein but also the outside world. The Iranians had made it clear that they wanted to export their Islamic revolution to other Islamic states. They had also turned their backs on most of the international community. Iran ignored concerns about human rights abuses. It was antagonistic toward Western powers and Arab nations alike. It also supported terrorists. (Five bombs planted by Iranian-linked terrorists exploded in Kuwait in December 1983. Among other things, they targeted the U.S. and French embassies.)

Then, late in 1983, Iran alarmed the rest of the world even more by threatening to close the Strait of Hormuz. This narrow passageway offers the only entry into the Persian Gulf. At the time, approximately 70 percent of Japanese, 50 percent of western European, and 7 percent of American oil imports came from the gulf.

The Iranian threat was a response to Iraq's air attacks on its Kharg Island oil refinery. The Iranians believed those attacks had been carried out with foreign-supplied arms. Khomeini said in a speech on September 19, "If they [the major Western powers] help Saddam to attack our economic resources, they will not see any more oil."

Ironically, Khomeini's threat played right into the hands of Saddam Hussein.

CHAPTER 4

THE TANKER WAR AND THE WAR OF THE CITIES

As early as May 1981, Iraq declared that all ships heading to or returning from Iranian ports in the northern zone of the Persian Gulf could be attacked. Several Iranian merchant ships and some ships from neutral nations were hit during this time. Iraq used French-made Exocet missiles launched by Iraqi helicopters or Iraqi jet fighters.

Then in 1984, Hussein seemed to realize that a threat to shipping in the Persian Gulf might draw the rest of the world into the war. That, in turn, might lead to more pressure on Iran to end it. Moreover, attacking shipping offered him hope for some much-needed military success. His army and people were tired of the war. A few victories would help his propaganda campaign.

A Line of Death

And so, in March 1984, Iraq established a 700-foot (1,126-km) "maritime exclusion zone." Iraq warned that any shipping coming into the zone was subject to attack. The line reached from the mouth of the Shatt al Arab to the Iranian port of Bushehr. Attacks against international shipping happened almost immediately. On April 18, 1984, an Iraqi missile struck a small Panamanian tanker near Kharg Island.

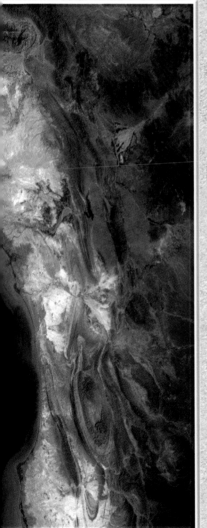

A view of the Strait of Hormuz, photographed from the space shuttle *Challenger* in April 1984. In response to Iraqi attacks on international shipping in the Persian Gulf, Iran threatened to close the Strait of Hormuz in the early 1980s.

Over the rest of the year, Iraq attacked more than seventy merchant ships.

Iran responded by attacking merchant ships headed to or from Iraq. In April, it shelled an Indian freighter. In May, it attacked first a Kuwaiti oil tanker, then a Saudi tanker. However, Iran did not carry out its threat to close the Strait of Hormuz. The country had decided it needed open sea-lanes for its own oil exports.

These attacks came to be known as the "tanker war." The tanker war cut Iranian oil exports by 50 percent. It also reduced shipping in the gulf by one-quarter. Insurance rates for tankers increased. Persian Gulf oil deliveries slowed worldwide. However, Iran's mild response to Hussein's plan kept the Western powers from becoming directly involved in the war. That would take another two years. Hussein was now anxious, as the war had already cost him billions.

Iraq's Chemical Weapons Use

Back on land in October 1983, Iran launched Operation Dawn Four in the northern sector. This attack captured 250 square miles (647.5 sq km) of Iraqi territory. The Iranians held their ground against a counterattack by Hussein's elite Presidential Guard. However, the Iraqis used mustard gas in the attack. This was the first confirmed use of chemical weapons by the Iraqis; it wouldn't be the last.

In the First World War (1914–1918), chemical weapons caused an estimated 1.3 million casualties, including 90,000 deaths. The Geneva Protocol of 1925 banned the use of such weapons. Both Iran and Iraq had agreed to abide by that protocol.

From the very beginning of the Iran-Iraq War, Iran claimed Iraq was using both mustard gas and tabun, a nerve gas. By February 16, 1984, Iran claimed it knew of forty-nine instances of chemical warfare attacks in forty border areas. The attacks had killed 109 people and injured hundreds more. That same day, Iran launched a major offensive. Over the next month, Iran claimed Iraq used chemical weapons at least fourteen more times, wounding another 2,200 people.

The United Nations (UN) verified at least one such attack soon afterward. The UN also found reasons to believe other Iranian allegations. On March 30, 1984, the United Nations Security Council issued a statement condemning the use of chemical weapons. That same day, the United States announced it was instituting special licensing requirements for exports to Iraq and Iran of chemicals that could be used in the manufacture of chemical weapons. It urged other governments to do the same. Many did.

After the resolution, reports of Iraqi chemical warfare declined, but they did not stop. And in 1987 and 1988, the Iraqi Kurds were punished for their rebellion against Hussein by attacks using mustard gas, cyanide, and tabun. Thousands were killed and many thousands more injured. The worst attack came in March 1988, on the Kurdish town of Halabja. Five thousand men, women, and children were killed, and nearly 10,000 were injured.

The 1984 Campaigns

Early in 1984, Iran again said it was determined to overthrow the Baath regime. Iraq responded by naming eleven Iranian cities it said it would attack if Iran launched another offensive. On February 7, 1984, Iran carried out a probing attack in the north. Iraq attacked the Iranian cities as promised. Iran responded in kind. Iraq suspended its air strikes on February 22. By then it was obvious that bombing Iranian cities would not stop the Iranian attacks. On February 15, the Iranians had launched another massive assault.

This assault resulted in the largest battle yet. Half a million men fought along a 150-mile (241-km) front. The Iranian regular army planned the attack, but most of the fighters were from the Iranian Revolutionary Guard Corps and Basij. In all, the battle claimed 25,000 lives.

The first part of the offensive occurred between February 15 and 24. Its aim was to cut the Baghdad-Basra highway and capture the key town of Kut al-Amara. Iranian forces managed to seize some strategic high ground about 15 miles (24 km) from the highway. On February 24, a second stage of the offensive was launched toward Basra. The attack took place over marshland the Iraqis had thought impassable. For a while it looked like Iran would finally manage to breach the Iraqi defenses. The Iranians did capture Majnoon Island, about 40 miles (64 km) north of Basra, in the heart of one of Iraq's richest oil fields. They held on to it despite vicious counterattacks (including the use of chemical weapons).

This photograph, taken on February 29, 1984, shows the aftermath of a series of clashes fought in the area between the Iraqi cities of Kut al-Amara and Basra. Between February 29 and March 1, the Iran and Iraq armies suffered more than 25,000 fatalities combined.

There were no major offensives for the next few months. Nevertheless, the war continued to claim lives. By June 1984, an estimated 900 civilians were being killed every week by attacks on cities. At the urging of United Nations secretary-general Pérez de Cuéllar, both sides agreed that month to halt attacks on urban centers. UN observers were placed in Baghdad and Tehran to act as monitors.

Ground combat in 1984 lessened across the front. Heavy rainfall hampered operations. In Tehran, much to everyone's surprise, the government was considering an Egyptian peace proposal. At the same time, Iran recaptured a few more square miles of territory it had lost to Iraq. Also, heavy but inconclusive fighting continued near Basra. However, there wasn't another major attack until January 28, 1985.

Operation Badr

The lull in fighting had allowed Iraq to build up its arms. It now had even greater military superiority. Iraq's January 1985 attack, however, did nothing against the Iranian army. Worse, even as Iraq launched its offensive, Iran was planning one of its own. On March 11, 1985, Iranian forces attacked toward Basra. This time, they abandoned human wave assaults in favor of more conventional warfare.

Code-named Operation Badr, the March 1985 offensive inflicted between 10,000 and 12,000 casualties on the Iraqis (the Iranians suffered 15,000). The Iranians finally succeeded in briefly capturing a portion of the

An unidentified Iranian walks past the body of a dead soldier in November 1985. The Al-Huweizeh marshlands, located east of Al-Qurnah, near the meeting of the Tigris and Euphrates Rivers, were the scene of a major push by Iranian forces into Iraqi territory.

Baghdad-Basra highway. But the war had long since become a bloodbath.

Civilian Attacks in the "War of the Cities"

Hussein responded to Operation Badr with the widest use of chemical weapons yet. He also resumed attacks on Iranian towns and cities. Iran responded in kind, in what became known as the War of the Cities. Its gains, meanwhile, were short-lived; its troops were driven back into the marshes.

The UN secretary-general again appealed for an end to the attacks on civilians. On April 6, 1985, both sides agreed. But on May 25, a suicide bomber attempted to kill the Kuwaiti monarch. Iraq blamed Iran and resumed bombing Iranian cities. Iran responded with missile attacks on Baghdad.

The ground war had settled back into a stalemate, but air attacks continued on both cities and industrial complexes. Iraq then attacked Kharg Island several times between August and December. Iran responded with yet more attacks on towns, cities, and maritime shipping. The give-and-take was wearing on troops, civilians, money, and the two governments.

Another Peace Offer

On February 9, 1986, Iran launched Operation Dawn 8. This was a three-pronged attack using more than 200,000 troops. Two parts of the attack were directed to the north and south of Basra. The third was aimed at the Fao

Peninsula, farther to the south. Iran captured the peninsula in less than a day and held it against the heavy Iraqi counter-attacks. Casualties numbered in the tens of thousands on both sides.

Next, Iranian forces broke out of the Fao Peninsula toward Umm Qasr. Capturing the port would have severed Iraq from the gulf. Although Iraq halted the attack, Iran's capture of the peninsula was still a huge victory. The Iranian forces made further gains over the next few months. They eventually moved artillery to within 10 miles (16 km) of Basra, allowing them to shell it at will.

To counteract the impact on morale of the Fao offensive, Hussein launched an attack in May that captured 60 square miles (155 sq km) around the Iranian town of Mehran. He then offered to withdraw if Iran would withdraw from Fao. Instead, Iran drove out the Iraqis within two months.

Hussein must have felt threatened by the Iranian successes. On August 3, 1986, he sent an open letter to the Iranian leadership. In it, he said his main condition for peace was now the security of his own regime. When Iran rejected his offer, reiterating that he had to be overthrown, Hussein lashed out with the most ferocious aerial campaign of the war so far.

He launched more attacks on Kharg Island and on major Iranian cities, including Tehran. On August 12, 1986, Iraq bombed the oil terminal on Sirri Island. Located 150 miles (241 km) north of the Strait of Hormuz, Sirri

Iranian soldiers ride past the bodies of Iraqi soldiers at the oil port of Faw, Iraq, in February 1986. Iran claimed it was successfully fending off Iraqi counterattacks as its armies made advances into Iraqi territory across the Shatt al Arab waterway.

Island had been thought out of Iraq's range. Hussein proved that it wasn't.

But the Iranians remained unbowed. In April 1986, Ayatollah Khomeini had issued a fatwa (religious ruling) instructing his forces to win the war by March 21, 1987, the Iranian New Year's Day. With that goal in mind, the Iranians launched yet another major offensive toward Basra on December 24, 1986. Planned and executed by the speaker of the Iranian Parliament, Ali Akbar Hashemi Rafsanjani, the massive night attack was intended to overwhelm the Iraqi defenders. Instead, the attack failed completely. Superior Iraqi firepower killed 10,000 Iranians in three days.

The Iranians attacked again in the same region in January 1987. They seized some territory but failed yet again to break through the main Iraqi lines. When the Iranian New Year rolled around, they still hadn't won the war. In fact, the January attack proved to be their last large offensive.

CHAPTER 5

THE TIDE TURNS

In the Persian Gulf, the tanker war was going badly for the Iranians. Late in 1986, Iran had intensified its attacks, especially on Kuwaiti ships. Kuwait asked both the United States and the Soviet Union to help protect its tankers. In early 1987, Kuwait chartered three tankers from the Soviet Union that flew the Soviet flag.

The United States was hesitant, but on May 17, 1987, an Iraqi missile hit the USS *Stark*, killing thirty-seven crew members. Baghdad apologized for the attack. Washington blamed Iran for escalating the war. The United States agreed to provide escorts for eleven Kuwaiti tankers, provided they flew the U.S. flag and were crewed by Americans.

Iran had mined much of the gulf. Several ships had struck the mines, including a Soviet freighter, one of the Soviet tankers leased by Kuwait, and, on July 22, 1987, one of the Kuwaiti tankers flying the U.S. flag. In retaliation, the United States destroyed an Iranian ship it had caught laying mines. Then, in early October, U.S. naval helicopters sank three Iranian patrol boats the United States claimed had fired on them. Soon after, one of Iran's Chinese-made Silkworm missiles struck a U.S.-flagged tanker. This time the United

On May 17, 1987, an Iraqi jet fired an Exocet missile at the USS *Stark*; the attack left thirty-seven crew members dead. Three days later, as shown here, smoke was still rising from onboard fires.

The Iran-Contra Affair

In 1985, several Americans were being held hostage by Lebanese terrorists with links to Iran. After some hostages were released at the request of Rafsanjani, the speaker of the Iranian Parliament, President Ronald Reagan sent a secret message to Rafsanjani thanking him for his efforts. He then authorized Robert McFarlane, his National Security Council adviser, to explore the possibility that Tehran might influence the Lebanese terrorists to free the seven Americans they still held hostage in "probable" exchange for American weapons.

President Ronald Reagan *(left)* steps down from the podium as Attorney General Edwin Meese prepares to answer press corps questions at the White House on November 25, 1986.

On September 13, 1985, Iran received 508 American-made antitank missiles through a third country. The next day an American hostage was freed. The United States continued to sell weapons to Iran for some time, but no other American hostages were released. Proceeds from the sales were routed to anti-Communist forces (known as contras) fighting in Central America. The deal became public knowledge in November 1986. The resulting controversy became known as the Iran-Contra Affair (or "Irangate").

In a speech on March 4, 1987, President Reagan admitted that what he originally saw as a strategic opening toward better relations with Iran deteriorated into "trading arms for hostages."

"There are reasons why it happened but no excuses," he said. "It was a mistake."

States destroyed two offshore oil installations. It also destroyed Iranian military radar and antiaircraft guns.

Iran's failures and defeats on land and at sea added to economic problems caused by the war and the mounting casualties. All had by now deeply affected Iranian military and public morale. Volunteers for the army became scarce, hurting the military effort. In an attempt to push Iranian morale even further downhill, Hussein launched his heaviest attacks yet on civilian targets in late February 1988.

Over a two-month period, more than 200 surface-to-surface missiles and other air raids struck Iran's major cities. Government employees joined the general public in fleeing Tehran. The Iranian government became paralyzed. The war was becoming insupportable for the Iranians.

In April 1988, the U.S. frigate *Samuel B. Roberts* was severely damaged by a mine. American ships responded by destroying two Iranian oil rigs. Also sunk or damaged were six Iranian vessels, including two of Iran's three naval frigates.

That same month, Iraq went on the offensive. In just forty-eight hours, the Iraqis recaptured the Fao Peninsula. At the end of May, they drove the Iranians out of their positions east of Basra. In June, they recaptured Majnoon Island. On July 13, Iraq threatened to invade southern Iran unless Iran immediately withdrew all its remaining forces from Kurdistan. Iran complied the following day.

At the beginning of June, Rafsanjani was named commander in chief of the Iranian armed forces, replacing President Ali Khamenei. Some Iranian clerics began lobbying Ayatollah

Khomeini to end the war. If it went on much longer, they argued, it might endanger Khomeini's Islamic revolution itself.

Then, on July 3, 1988, the American cruiser, USS *Vincennes* fired a missile at and shot down Iran Air Flight 655. Crewmen aboard the cruiser mistook the airliner for an attacking F-14 fighter. The attack killed 290 passengers and crew. The tragedy gave Iran the reason it needed to end hostilities while letting it save face.

Mourners carry coffins through the streets of Tehran on July 7, 1988, four days after the USS *Vincennes* accidentally shot down Iran Air Flight 655, killing all 290 people aboard. Soon after, Khomeini agreed to a diplomatic solution to end hostilities with Iraq.

Cease-Fire Negotiations

Ayatollah Khomeini read a statement at a meeting of the Iranian leadership on July 16, 1988. In it he indicated his willingness to accept a diplomatic solution to the eight-year war. Less than two months earlier, in a speech on May 28, he had said that the "fate of the war would be decided on the battlefields and not at the negotiating table." Things had obviously changed for the embattled leader. The assembly approved Khomeini's statement. The destruction of Iran Air Flight 655, Rafsanjani told them, proved that America would not let Iran win the war.

On July 18, 1988, Iran announced that it would unconditionally accept United Nations Security Council Resolution 598. The resolution, which had been passed a year earlier provided guidelines for a cease-fire.

But Saddam Hussein rejected this first Iranian acceptance of the cease-fire. He demanded that Ayatollah Khomeini explicitly and publicly endorse the resolution in person. To back up his demand, Hussein launched a series of air raids against important industrial plants on July 18. Iraq also attacked Iran's nuclear reactor in Bushehr. Iran struck back, but it could no longer match Iraq's military might.

On July 20, 1988, Khomeini issued a statement, read by an announcer on the Islamic republic's official radio station. In it, Khomeini accepted the UN resolution, but called it "more bitter than poison." He went on to say, "Had it not been in the interests of Islam and Muslims, I would never have accepted this, and would have preferred death and martyrdom instead."

Hussein still wasn't satisfied. The resolution called for a cease-fire before negotiations began. Iraq insisted on peace talks first, then a cease-fire. Haggling went on for three weeks, while military clashes continued. They included a full-blown invasion by Mujaheddin e-Khalq, Iranian dissidents based in Baghdad. With support from the Iraqi military, the Mujaheddin e-Khalq drove 90 miles (145 km) into Iran before being decisively defeated by the Iranian Revolutionary Guard Corps. The attack prompted brutal suppression of the remnants of Mujaheddin e-Khalq in Iran.

The countries that had backed Hussein in the war pressured him to accept the cease-fire. On August 6, Hussein finally agreed. By that time, he had once again alienated the countries that had supported him. On August 8, the UN Security Council declared a cease-fire effective at dawn on August 20. Iraqi and Iranian representatives would begin negotiations on August 24. A 350-strong force of UN military observers was created to monitor the cease-fire. The U.S. secretary of defense, Fran Carlucci, announced that the United States would soon reduce its presence in the gulf.

Suddenly, the war was over. After eight years of fighting and more than a million casualties, the borders of the two countries remained unchanged.

Peace Talks and War Legacy

The peace talks began on schedule. For two years they dragged on. Hussein again insisted on full control of the

Shatt al Arab. Iran insisted on the re-establishment of the 1975 Algiers Accord.

Then, in the summer of 1990, Iraq suddenly gave in, agreeing to honor the borders specified in the Algiers Accord and to pay Iran $25 billion in war reparations. On August 21, 1990, Iraqi forces withdrew from the 920 square miles (2,383 sq km) they still occupied in Iran, and prisoners of war were finally exchanged.

Iraq had good reason to finally settle with Iran. Saddam Hussein had just invaded another neighboring country, Kuwait.

The following spring, a coalition of forces led by the United States drove the Iraqis from Kuwait. Part of the cease-fire agreement was a promise on Iraq's part to disarm itself of chemical weapons and dismantle its efforts to produce nuclear weapons, and to allow UN inspectors to verify that disarmament. Its failure to live up to that agreement led to the removal of Saddam Hussein's regime by another United States-led military coalition in the spring of 2003.

Ayatollah Khomeini died in June 1989. His successor as supreme leader is Ali Khamenei, president of Iran and commander in chief of its armed forces during the war.

Exactly what relations will be like between Iran and post-Hussein Iraq remains to be seen.

armor Armored vehicles, such as tanks.

artillery Large-caliber weapons, such as cannons and missile launchers, that are operated by crews.

ayatollah Means "sign of God"; a leading expert in Islamic law.

Baath Socialist Party A political party, advocating Arab nationalism and economic socialism, that ruled Iraq during the Iran-Iraq War and continued to do so until recently.

chemical weapons Devices that release a toxic chemical designed to kill or maim, or the toxic chemical itself.

coup Short for coup d'état, the sudden overthrow of a government, usually by a small group of persons who hold or used to hold positions of authority.

imam Until it was applied to Khomeini, for Twelver Shiites, one of the twelve successors to the Prophet descended from Ali; in Arabic, any learned cleric.

infantry Soldiers armed and trained to fight on foot.

Islam A world religion founded by the prophet Muhammad in the seventh century.

Kurds A group of people who inhabit northern Iraq and Iran, with a culture distinct from the Arabs and Persians who make up the majority of the population in those countries.

mullah A Muslim cleric or preacher.

Muslim One who follows the religion of Islam.

mustard gas A chemical weapon that burns the skin and mucous membranes and causes severe, sometimes fatal respiratory damage; first used during the First World War and also used by Iraq during the Iran-Iraq War.

purge To eliminate people who are considered unsuitable or undesirable from an organization or government.

regime A government in power.

shah The king of Iran.

Shiism The smaller of the two main branches of modern Islam, made up of descendants of people who backed the prophet Muhammad's nephew, Ali, as successor to the Prophet after the Prophet's death in 632.

Sunnism The larger of the two main branches of modern Islam, made up of descendants of people who accepted a leader from outside the Prophet's family after his death in 632.

tabun A nerve gas used by Iraq during the Iran-Iraq War.

thalweg The line defining the lowest points along the length of a riverbed or valley.

ORGANIZATIONS

American Kurdish Information Network
2600 Connecticut Avenue NW, Suite#1
Washington, DC 20003-1558
e-mail: akin@kurdistan.org
Web site: http://www.kurdistan.org

Foundation for Iranian Studies
4343 Montgomery Avenue
Bethesda, MD 20814
e-mail: fis@fis-iran.org
Web site: http://www.fis-iran.org

The Iraq Foundation
1012 Fourteenth Street NW, Suite 1110
Washington, DC 20005
e-mail: iraq@iraqfoundation.org
Web site: www.iraqfoundation.org

Web Sites

Due to the changing nature of Internet links, the Rosen Publishing Group, Inc., has developed an online list of Web sites related to the subject of this book. This site is updated regularly. Please use this link to access the list:

http://www.rosenlinks.com/wcme/iriw

Cartlidge, Cheres. *Iran*. San Diego, CA: Lucent Books, 2002.

Gordon, Matthew. *Ayatollah Khomeini*. Broomall, PA: Chelsea House Publishers, 1991.

Korzine, Phyllis. *Iraq*. San Diego, CA: Lucent Books, 2003.

Schaffer, David. *The Iran-Iraq War*. San Diego, CA: Lucent Books, 2003.

Shields, Charles J. *Saddam Hussein*. Broomall, PA: Chelsea House Publishers, 2002.

Spencer, William. *Islamic Fundamentalism in the Modern World*. Brookfield, CT: Millbrook Press, 1995.

BIBLIOGRAPHY

Chubin, Shahram, and Charles Tripp. *Iran and Iraq at War*. Boulder, CO: Westview Press, 1988.

Hiro, Dilip. *The Longest War: The Iran-Iraq Military Conflict*. New York: Routledge, 1991.

Karsh, Efraim. *The Iran-Iraq War 1980–1988*. Oxford, England: Osprey Publishing, 2002.

Moin, Baquer. *Khomeini: Life of the Ayatollah*. New York: Thomas Dunne Books, 1999.

Schaffer, David. *The Iran-Iraq War*. San Diego, CA: Lucent Books, 2003

INDEX

About the Author

Edward Willett is a writer living in Canada.

Photo Credits

Cover, pp. 8, 14, 18 © Bettmann/Corbis; pp. 1, 3, 22, 26–27, 28, 31, 32 © Francoise de Mulder/Corbis; pp. 4–5 © Reuters New Media Inc./Corbis; p. 11 © Hulton-Deutsch Collection/Corbis; pp. 6–7 (both maps) courtesy of the Perry-Castãnedia Library Map Collection/The University of Texas at Austin; p. 16–17 © Setboun/Corbis; pp. 38–39 © NASA/Corbis; p. 43 © Pavlovsky Jacques/Corbis; pp. 45, 48, 50–51, 54 © AP/World Wide Photos; p. 52 © Bod Daugherty/AP/World Wide Photos.

Designer: Nelson Sá; **Editor:** Mark Beyer;
Photo Researcher: Nelson Sá